Here's what people are saying about Critics of Mystery Marvel

"Youssef Alaoui's poems in *Critics of Mystery Marvel* are the exoskeletons of bullets, of bombs. Be careful, but proceed anyway. The barrage is not for harm, but for diversion: It is hiding a deep pool where lightning gathers in a broken heart, where silver shards of memory rise painful, but sweet in this poet's voice. 'If only my five fingers were dynamite/for when 'I touched you I discovered/ your heart is a dark and gorgeous mountain... If we meet again/ and if I should hold you /this mountain will shudder and crumble.'"

—Dian Sousa, author of
Lullabies for The Spooked and Cool (2004) and
The Marvels Recorded in My Private Closet (2014)

"The Maghrebi artist is naturally surreal, as Algerian poet Habib Tengour says, and thus also 'always elsewhere. And that is where he fulfills himself.' As Youssef Alaoui does here, creating a poetry that uses his surrealist Maghrebi gaze to poke holes & illuminate the basic American Reel — & vice-versa. Fez shimmers in the Bay Area, and the Bay Area is a Fazi's Fata Morgana. But you can touch it all, because it lives in the solid everyday real of these poems."

—Pierre Joris, author of *Barzakh: Poems 2000-2012* (2014)

"I have been following this wonderful poet-magician for a long time and have always admired how he continues to cross boundaries. In this new collection we're taken on a tour of a complex and delightful mind."

—Neeli Cherkovski, author of
Elegy For My Beat Generation (2018)

T0083785

CRITICS OF MYSTERY MARVEL

CRITICS OF
MYSTERY MARVEL

YOUSSEF ALAOUI

COLLECTED POEMS

Introduction by Laila Halaby

2LEAF PRESS

NEW YORK

www.2leafpress.org

P.O. Box 4378
Grand Central Station
New York, New York 10163-4378
editor@2leafpress.org
www.2leafpress.org

2LEAF PRESS
is an imprint of the
Intercultural Alliance of Artists & Scholars, Inc. (IAAS),
a NY-based nonprofit 501(c)(3) organization that promotes
multicultural literature and literacy.
www.theiaas.org

Cover art: Amine Alaoui-Fdili
Cover design: Youssef Alaoui
Book design and layout: Gabrielle David
Poetry editor: Sean Dillon

Library of Congress Control Number: 2017963104

ISBN-13: 978-1-940939-66-7 (Paperback)
ISBN-13: 978-1-940939-80-3 (eBook)

10   9   8   7   6   5   4   3   2   1

Published in the United States of America

First Edition | First Printing

2LEAF PRESS trade distribution is handled by University of Chicago Press / Chicago
Distribution Center (www.press.uchicago.edu) 773.702.7010. Titles are also available
for corporate, premium, and special sales. Please direct inquiries to the UCP Sales De-
partment, 773.702.7248.

To the critics of mystery marvel

CONTENTS

VERILY, WE LIE / 5

THOUGHT FORM / 17

NAKED BONES / 29

UNTRUTHISMS / 43

ALONE
PARIS REAPING / 55

SHELL—SHOCKED / 77

ANACHRONIST / 95

ZELIJ, A MAZE / 107

BRIAR & POND / 123

SPILLING OVER / 137

ACKNOWLEDGMENTS

Some of these pieces first appeared in Andrei Codrescu's *Exquisite Corpse, Big Bridge, Full of Crow, Red Fez, the San Luis Obispo New Times Weekly,* Michael Boughn's *Resist More/Obey Little,* and the films of Audio Visual Terrorism.

Special thanks to Marie L., Aldo Robinson, Yuri Zambrano, and Henrik Aeshna for their assistance in the translations.

Extra special thanks to tonton Amine Alaoui-Fdili of Casablanca, Morocco, for his beautiful painting on the cover. ✸

INTRODUCTION

I RECEIVED AN EMAIL ASKING if I would write an introduction to a book of poetry by a poet I'd never heard of. Youssef Alaoui is half Moroccan but not known to the Arab writing community, I was told. "I think it is important for an Arab American poet to write the introduction, sort of to indoctrinate him into this community of writers, and I think it would be fitting if it was a woman (I am pro-woman). So I thought of you," Gabrielle David wrote.

She said that she would need the introduction in two weeks.

I said yes even though I was so busy I had stopped breathing.

Turns out that for reasons of writing or circumstance or timing of mystery, *Critics of Mystery Marvel* was that very right CPR moment, that BOOM! THUMP! POW! to restart the breathing.

Let the critics of mystery marvel.

I was stuck on the title though and kept reading it with different understandings. Was that the intention? Was *Marvel* a noun or a verb? Was there a superhero reference I was missing? (Is that why I kept thinking in BOOMs and POWs?) I needed to know. And so Youssef and I had a conversation for clarity.

That conversation was another THUMP! followed by a long, clean breath.

I marvel.

∽

WE LOVE TO CATEGORIZE EACH OTHER and while yes, Youssef Alaoui is an Arab American poet or a Latino Moroccan poet, he is very much an American poet. His knowledge of American culture is intimate—of course it is; he has lived his life here—his love of rock and roll is passionate, and his words are flavored with French, Spanish, and Arabic. Poems like "Watergate" and "Coney Island Siren" illustrate that how you see is not always how you are seen and how you are seen is not necessarily how you see.

Youssef is intrigued by the mysteries not just in life and love but also the deeper, darker stuff that's wedged into the suitcases of every family and every mind; he picks through it all and renders his discoveries in unexpected and often lovely and very diverse visuals — squirming pigeons and ships and slivers. Here is a sensitive man who pays attention to dreams and feelings, who states "I like madness and things that happen inside the mind," and while it must be exhausting in there, we reap the benefits of his studiousness. In this meaty collection, you will find poems of the brain as well as poems of the heart, all of which pulse through with a slow, steady beat.

Count it out.

When I asked him how it could be that poems that are structurally and topically so different are clearly written by the same person, he attributed it to rhythm, suggesting that his relationship to music is present in his poems. I wonder if it is also connected to the ocean, which he can see from his place of writing.

Critics of Mystery Marvel is a lyrical and sensual collection that rakes through intimacies and disappointment with fearlessness and deep thought: language as a toy, love viewed from a thousand and one angles, places that cannot be claimed except in dreams and memory. These poems are the anticipation of a first kiss...bare feet padding into a living room...sex for the last time with the person you love most.

Farid Matuk (another Arab Latino American poet) speaks about the lack of Arab intimacy accessible in the American world of media, something to the effect of "We see defiled and violent Arab bodies, but not intimate ones." Perhaps because I am a woman I had not noticed this missingness, or perhaps because I am not a man of color I had missed some of the nuances of the self-hatred that is taught in so many of our systems. An African American friend told me that when she was a teenager growing up in the suburbs she was terrified of black men because she only knew them from the news where they did horrible things or were dead. Youssef Alaoui has bridged this struggle of not finding himself present in his own culture except in negatives, and then finding his own positives among those negatives.

∽

BACK TO THE TITLE.

It is important to revel in the mysteries that life presents us, Youssef explains. "When mystery appears between cultures, fear is often the result. We should no longer fear mystery. We should allow ourselves to be enchanted by it instead."

We should marvel. ✹

—Laila Halaby
April, 2018

VERILY, WE LIE

Once, a Bird

Daddy pulled a dried baby bird from his ear, once. We were gathered around the table, chewing on corn flakes. He tried to hide it in a napkin, then his lap, but I noticed. He took us to the park that afternoon. I watched his eyes well up with tears while he gazed at the trees.

Tango of Knives

When first we met
we would dance very close

holding sharpest knives
poised to strike

till sun rose again
to glint the blades.

Once, you licked your lips
stroking the handle of a cleaver.

I smiled and sliced
the music down.

Those were sweet days.
Recently, someone did stab your heart.

Sorry it wasn't me.

Circumstances

Today
I drive to your house
but never seem to get there.

Late afternoon
I kiss your nicotine lips.
It's the closest I get
to smoking anymore.

Tonight
we sleep in sheets I gave you.
Your body still feels linked to mine
I don't know why.

Tomorrow
I put this all behind me.
Will you?

Miles to Go Before I Sleep

Christmas again.
I watch you pour the wine
in large gestures
as if it were viscous.

You like to think you're fancy.
I think of how you will use
your large gestures

later tonight
once we are alone.
I smile

and put my keys
in the fish bowl.

These woods are lovely
dark and deep.

Immortal Desirous

Fifty *FUCK!s* in the car alone
slamming my hand
against the wheel, radio blaring

Speeding down a dark
tree-lined highway without headlights
still can't erase that feeling

Complicit, you promised
to forget me. The ache
was so sweet, we had to

The grinding of our heavy bones
lit sparks beneath the sheets.

Yours to Look at Forever

Sprites scattered the living room
when I entered this morning.

Emptiness filled it
as if everyone stopped talking.

I will buy that bus ticket today.
And marriage? Take this photo.
Place it somewhere.

Your favorite mirror.
I will hover among layers
of face powder and memory.

Your window.
I will float in tree limbs
and storm clouds.

It's Only the Wind, You Say
Camping in the Sahara

But what of the millions of molecules
fusing and separating, what of
the wind they whisper about on calm nights
that makes rocks wander and lifts horses

Or flashing pelts of rain and hail
with sprawling torrents that topple
skull-shattering boulders
to crush houses and fill valleys

What of the churning chaos
the massive waves of nothingness
falling into one another
sweeping up heaven and land
dispersing it over the defenseless

I'm dead serious
as you look at me your eyes
grow deep and playful, your posture softens
you shift slightly, limbs warm
half under the covers

Then the wind howls
like a giant dog who sings to the moon
Then he eats the moon and it becomes his eye

Now the empty night is his glassy black fur
and we are fleas, once sunk deep in his coat
recently knocked back to the sand

All we can do (to pester the dog)
is burn tiny embers

The sparks of our fire
raise sideways, dimly, randomly
and stop when they meet his hide

THOUGHT FORM

Beware the Day

One calm summer morning
I see the white buses arrive.

Five men stop our group
to say we must take
a combination of pills and
vaccines for oncoming illness.

They take some themselves.
I don't. I have to sneak away.

I run a straight line
away from them
following the shadow
of a telephone pole.

This Boy Is a Sword

I am held at gunpoint with a group of people in a room. Pistol at my neck, surrounded by kidnappers pointing pistols at me. People I know try to barge through the door. Unsuccessful. Some get through. A young Toshiro Mifune among them. He forces his way to a table where he eats a sandwich with overplayed gusto, pressed in a crowd of people hip height. We do not know our attackers. We bend and bleed anyway...

From a Snowy Place

Deep in my mind
I hear a piece of music
A snowy mountain folk song.

It is actually a coded recipe
For cooking human meat
Breaded and pan fried.

Suede Coat

Dream within a dream left me crying for fear that I had lost her. She is still there next to me. She says, *What's wrong? You haven't lost me. I'm right here.* I say, *You're beautiful. You're perfect. I'm going to lose you. I never want to lose you.* I look at her body. Her navel is perfect. Her hair is short. Her teeth are slightly pushed in. Hands perfect. Her feet are scraped, worn at the Achilles tendon. I say, *You like to wear heels, but they fuck with your feet.* Her big toe has a rash. *That's because you play basketball like a madman,* I tell her. *I swear this dream means I'm going to lose you. I don't want to lose you.*

Violin music appears. I look out a small window. Street musicians play outside, leaning up against the wall to our bedroom. I turn back. The bed is different. She's gone. Tabby cat asleep on the bed. I cover it with my suede coat. I know that a transformation is taking place. I've lost her. I lift the coat. It is worn on the lower back. The cat has changed. Orange now. I accept the change. The cat hops off the bed. I get dressed and put the coat on to smoke outside. I've seen her. And I have lost her again. Again I wake up. I am in my current body, in my current bedroom. My house is . . . my house. I put my clothes on, find my suede coat, and go outside to smoke at four-thirty in the morning, thinking about what has just happened.

The Soil

here

is a pile

of

fleshy goop

once

you weed

the lost traps

out of it

in order

to not disturb

the first thing

you must plant

is a nail

of pure

frozen

soil

Dead Letter Dream

Dawn lift blade blaze
I never heard the bold declare
of Laertes' sufficient realm to stay
long enough for cracking fear. A skill
quick killed in inversion scaling.

His hand hold, a force
toppled infant dagger coil.
Alas, no folds of iron curvature
remain blinded
by sweet apple memory.

A hunted deer coincided ad nauseam
with the death coin. Your answer please.
This is how deep we knelt.
A curious snake, not of consequence
tears the flesh
of a random pervert.

Ophelia hidden from above
this buzz, this muse
awakens—
to a fault.

Nightwater

Here is the dream. That one dream I had that one night. The one that woke me out of a deep sleep. I tried to tell you about it. You were in la-la land. Your mouth was hanging open. I drank some water for you.

So I had been drifting along when someone approached and said, *Hi, you remember this rock n' roll band, don't you?*

And I said, *Sure yeah I — Oh hey yeah! I remember you all from Portland, right?*

But no one else remembered — one of them shook her head. I left the room.

Then I remembered this dream I had, inside of my other dream. My memory of it was complete. Not like in the movies with folding cities and whatnot, running from one end of the screen to the other, whose limits of the imagination are maintained within a 16:9 ratio. This was pure, unadulterated, color scope dreaming swim time.

I remembered bouncing balls of granite in the kitchen, granite spheres, four feet tall, made to be mounted on architectural granite cones, but they had floated off their perch because spirits had possessed them, causing them to levitate. I did what I could to push them back down, but they bounced back up so whimsically, I started bouncing them.

I looked for the singer of that rock band I mentioned. He was in a room by himself, dressed as Frankenstein's monster, watching a horrid and deranged version of Frankenstein on television. The room was a terrible mess. I told him about the granite spheres. He believed me. I felt a tenderness between us. The monster on television was licking a woman to death. It was lewd. Her screams stopped our conversation. He turned off the television. I thought, *maybe he could take off his make up.* He looked so gentle without it. But perhaps I was attracted to him more when he looked like Frankenstein's monster.

Someone at the door. There had been an incident. He had to leave. *Stay here,* he said. I poured myself a drink from the counter. He was back minutes later. The séance had begun. *There is someone with us.* He took his costume blazer off. The light bulb blew out. I turned the ceiling light on. It went out. *Hey, would you turn a light on? Sure,* he said. Suddenly, we felt a downward force, like a terrible hurricane wind that tore at my clothes, shredding my jacket, and pulling at my arms. I could barely speak with no air in my lungs and the force twisted my face, but I managed to utter the word *STOP!* And that was when everything stopped.

NAKED BONES

Critics of Mystery Marvel

Your hair a flock of black goats
watering their lips
with my sister, a dove
every shallow lightning a tingle

In cabal we believe as soon
as we can, my brother
dust powder the torrent of knowledge
abandoned forever the simple

Harmonious mist laughing
an image so sublime
fertile treasure this too
is only dust, my horse

If grievance marches thus, versus
mirages fleeting where
every curtain lined with gauze
and smoke outside high curling

Then where the pace of hilltop crags
stands exposed and thirsting
in need of water clefts
you must speed on, my love

Past despair in human tones
then catch her vain boastings
in dawn blaze the sun
sword laden storm

Stacked in flame
the morning
casting jewels at the West
overflowing the cup
you must be there

I will

You Are Camera

You are camera flying into the sky
I am bird of wings horizon
We the watchers of wisdom lightning

This is our porous world
Careful steps on milky soil
Tap the one in spyglass puddle

Pure is now time
Melted and hollow
Now we sing the wish
Aloud

Bank of Dark Rails

Evening ghosts
Clutch the moon, won't let go
Belching engine
Spirit trees
Wake me determined to convince

Heron flies of stone not soil
Rails don't fall from the sky
Cutting a path through the shrubs
Through the trees, through them

Hordes of bushes slipping to the river
If a lake comes up you must name it
Every lake, every time
No lake has no name

Monument Rock Witness

Tilted sun bled red
Self slips into new self
Caught between maker and maudlin
Daytime after parties fill the spiderweb
Curtains made for nothing
Losing surely hungry people
This charge will resolve a sky
Albeit iron-stained

Lost in Rhododendron Dells

Blindfolded, silent, you took me wandering
holding hands, ducking under branches

When unmasked at last, you presented
an unseen place, hunkering us in a bush of flowers

No time to kiss, these visions groove down
hard, etching on a young brain, quick who's next

To lead, to follow, to wonder
if the rhododendrons noticed you gone.

Crystal Lass

Dew frost crust her eyelids
brought morning down with a shock

cooling tides in night quiet parted
our invaded cities emptied

revealing her corpse
between trash bin and car bumper
in a small lot

dragged there by capillary action, perhaps as
the night froze around her

it was the last gesture she had to give
yet not as brilliant
as she ever gave.

To the Lights of B'Way
Summer of Hell NYC, 2005

Because Lord I love thy crystal lights
and glad they blind me, gazing upon 'em.
Signals for all their flaxen luster
of Pure Identity, which I seek, and so cherish.

Were these brazen gems to lose their flash
t'would mean the very edge
of Destiny's fabric had lost its weave
to leave me beached in a wake of annihilation.

Because I am not Parisian.

Paris, screaming, beneath the blighted rump
of a demon ape forged of flame itself
pleads to her rivers for help
and squanders her most sainted hands

As humble bargaining chips
for the knotted fist of Abraxas.
Those who remain pray it is enough
while their Pope hunkers, rummaging for clouds.

The World Found Me

Where day flames a new world
traced with creaks and
cackles in roaring glades

A silken cake pedestal
spreads a quilt between four hills
draining into caverns below
gentle rolls of backdrop tree dew
mussed by glitter breeze

He says
she sells
sea shoulders over crystal sands
in clearest water
clear enough to fall forever into

So sleepy now
ready to die in plump comfort claws
a nest you beaked for me
empanada y soda
pioneer rails pulling away

Raking the guitar chords again
was it this
it was that glance you first gave me
loud trials I burn in secret

Monkey birds dive for cover
evening's violet eggshell canopy
edges of the dark earth slip
against wooden blocks in the mud
three curtains back
sits the wizard
no more me or
you

Colombia

If only my five fingers were dynamite
for when I touched you I discovered
your heart is a dark and gorgeous mountain.

If only the jungles hadn't overwhelmed us
I might have dug us a cave
to hide our lying bodies.

And if only we had savored the fruit we found
I'd have brought us a blanket
for the earth above is so cold.

If we meet again
and if I should hold you
this mountain will shudder and crumble.

UNTRUTHISMS

At Night on a Train

i.
We wander there
and get nowhere
as we fly past the rooftops

She's so high
we could touch the sky
we're lost on a train
in the city

ii.
Train doors reveal
cityscape tiled in ruins, cascades
multi-headed hydra tower
windows falling
stairs into walls

Train doors reveal
neon giant pinwheel, overstuffed panda
Coney Island love tunnel smells
like a thousand popcorn dinners
thrown up over years

Watergate

Once I was looking for rocks with you by the beach and I found one that looked like Henry Kissinger and then I found another one that looked just like Richard Nixon so *wow* I said to myself and then I found Bob Woodward and so the four of us decided we would reenact the entire Watergate Hotel Scandal right there on the beach but in salt water and rocks and driftwood walls with kelp wires then we got into an argument about who was going to leak the story first so I kicked the whole mess into the ocean and got a sunburn but when you blinked like that at me so slow I saw your eyelashes and forgot what I was doing.

Nightengale

El crepúsculo no me puede cuidar
de un afecto que parece desaparecerme
en esta noche húmeda.

La calavera de la mañana
con sus largos dedos rosados
fluirán silencios

Para estrangular las cimas
de los arboles (que están tan)
gigantes, fibrosos, y negrísimos

Con una luz repugnante
y un amor debilitante
que me aniquila.

En este momento
entre la noche ebria
y el amenecer enfermo

Entre el ruido de tu canción
y las venas coloradas
de nacimiento bifurcante
soy solo tuyo.

Ruiseñor
Tr. "Nightengale"

The tepid light cannot protect me
from an erasing affection
on this sweltering night.

The mad skeleton of morning
with her long, pink fingers
will flow silently

To strangle the tops
of the trees (they are so)
giant, black, and stringy

With a nauseating light
relative to that confusing feeling
that annihilates me.

At this moment
between the drunken night
and the morning arriving ill

Between the noise of your song
and the red veins
of another divided origination
I am yours alone.

Fall Has Fallen

grab
a pumpkin

make
sweet knife love
to its face

grab
the innards

stew them

and roast the seeds.

Chickenfoot

thanx

toots

god

's got
me

by
th' ankles

I
fly

but

the BLOOD
's rushing

to my head!

"Dubble-O" Pronounced "OO"

Or

*"Two Golden Eggs Clutch Each Other and
Float To The Sun"*

AH

Sweet golden pie, my crudest of lovelies.
Ours is a velvet-tone arena
rife with memory; polluted
by the sound of one another's voice.

OH

In the event of triviality
please touch my surface.
Our affection is blind
yet complete.

SO

Blind as the wooded winds
complete as the trumpet hill.
Final as the resonant bass
bellowing from the pit-darkened lake.

IT'S

Our greatest enemy.
Its thunder reveals our shadow
and threatens to bring us
back
to original nothingness.

YOU
But I believe
and I will
that our two may become
many more
than birds.

Considering the Following
Arrangement of Words

Sometimes humans
hold other humans
in witness of
peeling
banana wallpaper

ALONE
PARIS REAPING

Night Airplane Ride

Twilight descends the staircase
in a dark gown
with a trim of rose mist
dressing her tails
on smoky purple skies.

We approach the event horizon.

Now is night.
Catalog and display
of all the lonely places
lit up in tangerine dots
quilting the land
until the ocean.

Paris Metro

YOU! In the middle of a metro car! Your pockets are empty! No! They are full of dirt! No! They are full of granola scraps, leftover tobacco, and a small paper ticket! Turnstile! Blue score! White tile! Face the front of the train! Your face is a casket! The sallow morning mist carnage bellows a stunted sleep howl! You surf the train! You are no better than the train! Pass all the blurry heads! The brown-haired love letter leaves the car you once shared! It's better if you stand in the jointed section! Blood flows thicker in dreams! The bullet is not pointed! The plug is a prig! Step on the flowers! Headphone dance! Stand free! Plant your legs! An old man finishes his jelly donut, licks every part of his fingers, then wipes them on a support pole! Lean on that pole and watch the whole train squirm left, right, up and down like a worm, pulling itself through the earth.

Flowers for Edith Piaf

Death's head performance
rings down hills and foot trails this
ancient city was built upon.

Sundown brings sheets of
white fog pouring.
Cracked walls, stone alleys
drowning garden vines.

Dreams of deep
remorse, embarrassment.
How they made you sing.

Your flowers stay
where I left them
as they
take on evening's hue.

Now Drapes Close

God
winks from folds
in the studded sky

Now drapes close
somewhere the mirrors
a few lurking stars

Pointed rooftops
each pushes a window
into the sky

Beyond the highest loft
some round
between baroque curls

She dresses in black and gold
over clay tones
then undresses

Suicide is a sexy devil
who knows your name

God
winks from folds
in the studded sky

Now drapes close

Naked Twigs

Cackle in the eaves
each crow atop its own
eyeless demon crouched
rooftops launch behind them

Innards of a snail sky
some lacy ghost meat
blue-edged belly bag
clouds, a skirt of moss

Avenue twigs snapping hymns
downspout pours the gargle
eon bones push stone forever
rain, the gilded velvet coffin

Displays a diminished sun
pulled tight by sexy beast buttresses
immune, the observer settles
another evening of bitter herbs
in wine

Notre Dame Sunset

When the centuries-old cathedral
spawn of torture and tribulation

Stands bare-faced to witness the sun
enter his bed at the end of another day

Even after massive eons
soaked into the thousand eyes

Of her mask of saints
she blushes once again

Notre Dame II

Everything I own
under one arm

Static arcs over
shadow sidewalk

Leap from stones in the
hunchback's courtyard

Film grain in the air
stub your toe
on the righteous

I will sit here and watch
the colors deepen

Smoke the Roach of the Day

When all the day's pain and all the day's activities have been performed that can be performed and all the venom of the day coagulates into a concentration so thick it bears the common name of "sunset," things can get progressively worse. But forgive me to the fullest of bearable capabilities, for I am climbing ahead of myself, kicking my foot through the skin of my own paragraph.

Those precious last embers of the day shall, from here on, be referred to as the "roach" of the day. Once the teeth of itineraries have been plucked with iron tongs and the blood-spattered overgrowth of reckless sunlight has been wrapped up in a giant and mysteriously thin paper, the day is then smoked to its hilt. As the tars of day stick to twilight after sunset, thereby browning it, that is the roach.

When clouds mass on the horizon and toss around colors of the dying sun, it shall be said that the clouds are then smoking the roach of the day.

When humans stop what they're doing to witness it all, at available viewpoints dotted throughout their reality, they too smoke the roach of the day.

Although the following sad fact does not help us enjoy sunsets any further, it must be said that Parisians refer to depression as the "roaches," primarily at night. One might hope that the fruit and honey colors of the roach of the day might sweeten this idea somewhat, but Parisians are naturally heavy brooders, due to an excess of clouds and technical studies, and lacking in time taken away from the desk to participate in the spinning of the planet on its heavenly axis.

Lily Guild

Imagine
frozen waffles
frozen berry mix
empty sidewalks

Picture
frozen whipped cream
microwave syrup
hail outside

My window
my blankets
are yours

Train Direct to Your Chest

this chest of mine
box of squirming pigeons

rushing at the crumbs
my pulse rages over

staring at the neck plumes
inverted question marks

screams the velvet jugular
jagged line from the eye

the tunnel you wander is
lined with asphalt and blood gravy

upholstered in pain
only you can imagine it

I park my god cart there
looking for coins

When the Sky Swirls Stars That

Drip all the way to the ground
at the edge of your village
a dark midwinter walk and
silent snow phantoms approaching.

I call out to the last of you
leave my memory
much like that melody
we sang by the late fires
of final dawn, now
soap flakes and snow
fly the peacock-ridden balcony.

Tralala!
we hurled at the canyon
our voices embarrassed to be so slender
dwarfed by the rock blades
as the ribbed coast cut the air
even before we resigned to
shelter salt pillar brides.

The heart of it was so clear to me
you and I
filled with the stuff of all things
when last we spoke, but here
at the edge of your shadow
village I will turn
and take my chances
on faded trails.

No Handhold

My feet touched yours under the seat in front of me

Errant lovers they then increased in passion madness, yet
    so subtle for

She had married another and bore a child, mooned at the creature

In image, wind had rosed his cheek, lowered several locks

Over one sun trapped eye, it shone like a stone god

Borne of highest outcropping, the shiniest temples dedicated to

Sonorous bells chimed in honor where lambs laid bare

To trickle heart juices flowing over

Our feet touched and made such quick wet love

Dark struggles beneath the seat ahead, tangled

More than wishing over anything, like elbows braced in
    trampoline weekends

Criminal to behold, the clouds outside brooded in dark capes

Tall thunderheads illuminated from within, they raised a brow

But would not tell the jungle buttes beneath them

Spitting rain in heavy drops, they filled first the rivers and
    then the valleys

Our feet shook hands but would not ask for names

We lay still, buckled in respective chairs

Horizon spinning outside

Until the engines slowly stopped

Boule de Suif

Little Ball of Fat, Maupassant

Here in the snow-globe space
where light moves like jewel paste
in winter trees

So careful go the dead mountain wheels
view lace like this from uncovered cakes

Our fortune wears a lacquered box, we floating djinn
follow twin appaloosa velvet tide walkers

Across electric air and leaf paths
stretching in the darkened road forever

Sail the crescent beams of lantern glow
hidden spoils of dark mass festival

Desirous palates gloss the private arches gleaming
roast bird, plump fingers like sausages
an overwhelming bodice

Despised by your trap mates
locked behind curtained doors and soggy clouds

My eye strikes you opposite the fairy folk
indulging in your provisions

A circus round erupting later
spilling champagne, certain kerosene vampires
density silence, black cave memory

Finally, they have you
untied heathen, lamb-lipped, stony heart
frosty fire, the moist heat

Feeding frenzy stops when the jack-boot
slate-headed peacocks return to killing

They take what they always take
the weed-ridden honey

It means so little to the bear
and less to the bees that make it

But I watch you on our way out of there
and your swollen pigeons tremble
before dying in the mud, your bosom

No one would take
what you really had to give that day
nor could they, but we all grabbed anyway
and would rather kill you for it

Boule II

Wandering sounds between us
empire domes beneath us

Rhythm toads in log bent snow
a heartbeat fixed, a voyage taken

Or more, evasion requisitioned
ignoring skies saber-laden, rifles, collusion

I hold back from soft sheets the consequence
for disturbing locked doors, holiday asylum

Blood of Marat Boils
in the Bathwater

You, Marat
on considering passion
leave the notion padded and pansied.
You are only inviting knives —
shining, desirous, angry knives
letting them slip under the skirts of your ribcage
like so many Casanovas.

De Sade would have his way with you
could he reach you, back through time
from behind his bars.

He's drafting plays, you know.
Dreaming of tortures, spilling your blood
over and over, a smooth velvet elixir
into the bathwater that was to have cured you.
Splashing it over the breasts of France
all heaped up like a baby's bottom.

Remember that
inside or outside of Charenton
a man is only as mad
as his concept of madness will allow.

And Marat
your fantastical sciences
couldn't keep the people from your chest.
Nor did the Enlightenment

protect us from your politics.
And the greatest sum of your paper and doctrine
didn't make the killing any easier.

You offered us freedom couched in ideas.
You dictated an entire revolution from your bath.

It is written in a play for both you and De Sade:
We routed out the old tyrants, and now we have new tyrants.
But I still believe in revolution!

Marat—
this revolution has burned up everything in its path.
You promised us modernity from the ashes.

What we see in its place is blindness.
What was placed before us is displacement.
Now blinded and displaced, we are nothing!

The smoke of your revolution billows
with the aimless cinders
of freedom-lusting bodies
now peppering the landscape.

This is your sallow seed:
nothing but a wretched haze
occluding our vision and monotonizing
the voice of independence!

Was it your people who lit bonfires in the street?
I hate them. They keep me up at night.
And how did your song go? Was it sincere?
Ah, yes. I remember the words now.

They were so boring and trite!
You battered our heads with if and when!
Riddled our skulls with that insipid word
LIBERTÉ.

But we, smitten by the seduction of your revolution
and stupified by your logic, were deafened to the truth
as you pronounced your slogan
EGALITÉ.

Garbled as it was, bubbling up
from the stinking marsh of your mouth
our future hanging limp as you chewed it.
At last, you disclosed the final poison
coiled like a snake at the base of a tree
FRATERNITÉ.

After your greatest moment Marat
the one where you let it all go into your bath
the gendarmes stepped in
to let your precious lukewarm life soup
flow out from the base of the tub
and join with the rest of the Paris sewer water
coursing into the Seine, rushing to merge
with our nation's stretching jugular.

SHELL—SHOCKED

Deneb

The war raged on, ocean-like
tops of waves hankering to meet
and kill one another

God folding his arms
flicking his skirt
because he's a cat

People moaned and trod in droves
grinding their animals, smashing
never asking, never quitting

Squeezing life's slight tendrils
of flowing fiery motion
to pour it on the soil

Everyone, anyone, everywhere
forgetting their insignificance
giving it up to blood, to mud

Who cares anyway

Numbers Brain Game
Blinds the Spectator

sharp enticement vexes
throbbing chivalry smites

perfect sack sullies prisoner
capricious defense defies the master

vibrant vessel envelops
undisciplined guns wake the sleepless

tribal party shrieks unholy
lust enticement boils

rider goes ahead alone
upright battle-axe mars language

dark mass craves final
vibrant coma battalions awake

vestigial sheep drains complete
aggressive entry nags too soon

broken vein whispers bleak
sharp degeneration sheds

summer wars of the angry
perforated entry flows triumphant

Dog Fight

Asphalt river canyon walls
fasten in agitation
buzzer dust infusion cry
respect the crossly endless chain
of flailing fur and tail
glassy methadone wanderer
blacktop blur a ceaseless drive

Fang on hide then spin and curl
nay says I the mind of instruction
let these kill let blood let Haxan absolve
milk of thy wealth
read the fetid culture wound
indifference to danger
maniac jackal haunt

Prey on prey on preyed
pang of uneasiness
it's ecstasy unadulterated
on club nose skeleton claw
orgiastic carnage tide
when silver plated pools
sweep the city clean

Ruptured mud the useless
flutter banks boulder
over twig legs open wide
presence of the one
absence of the other
leak the clean death out let
sylvan gladness
in thrashes

Goodbye, My Soldier

He lowered his head, he left.
Weeks spiraled into months
in the smashed desert city.

He met a hundred families crying
starving, trapped, or fleeing.

Supplies dwindled.
His buddies held it together.
He knew love.

As the bullet entered his chest
he felt a sharp bruise

and knew
that god and the devil
were one.

Ramble Rumble,
Voices of the Aftermath

There will be no solution to this rhyme, not ever. Your cries have alighted the winter wind. Your eyes, your mind, the least of which you hold valuable, sob and sigh in the depths of night.

I will not count the grief built up of ages. We wander darkly. Taste this goal while warm…An automobile holds the answer…Somewhere, someone gasps for air. The times are trying. Stars stare through black space and wait for one truly concerned. They call blankly.

Remove all skin and leave the voice, for lips at this moment are useless. We, who would not behave, are trapped amongst the richest cavalcades of youth, funneling millennia, and glass tubes of rescue. Victim to any crime. Your solution will not render you useful. Your determination will crush us all.

I believe the one set to charge this solitary planet has given up the ghost. My poles wander aimlessly over the phone. I jaw. I rise. I giggle. The sex of later rabbits tore what nudism still contained. The drive is endless. The form is wan. The carrel is reformed. Meat still hangs on the dusty porch.

Ink Spiral Methuselah

I live so long, I'm alive when dead.
Ink spiral Methuselah smoking fat wads of tobacco
marijuana stogies wider than towel rolls
drinking moonshine of my youth
crawling worms overspill the cup.
O the joy
of a world slipping apart.

River jungles stuffed with candelabras
hanging low off bird monkey paths
under polished glass
vines, hairy chested ingots
build my throne tower of undead observation.

War.
A clean scientific theory that
naturally propagates accidental soldiers in its wake.

The passersby.
The bread bearers.
Home returners.
Makes civilians of soldiers.
Mush of heart.

The heaping dead need no clothes
no food, no smoke, no hurry.

Mouth full of cod and clay
dried stumps, my arms fold forever in pale dust
frozen thin mushroom lawns

cover mummy cloth gown
reaches stone cubes, interlocking
the floor of a machine gun tank
feeds my two stroke umber.

Scrying glass points at cloud swept ruins
screeching like a nest of cobra babies.

Sprawling almond vapor tundra valley
wagging keel obese time ship, hull burst
taking on air behind dullard cliffs
clicking away at amateur third degree rumination.

Hoping to wake in a gown of swords and
commit it all to paper for posterity
as if it were
some kind of graceful act
rather than a clumsy protracted murder
carried out with busking change
stuffed in a stinking sock
softening the back of a presidential skull
behind the locked and rusted dairy queen.

I am invisible to war
an embarrassment to blood.

The bats will never find me here.

Kung Fu Master Backward

Life in reverse is dance-like
problems resolve themselves
old flowers brighten
disappear into the earth

Bright puffs of light end with a bang
arrange the streets, open people's eyes
set them on their way

Zygote me dreams ethereal crowns
longing for a chance
to doubt you, to taste this moment

When blood settles back into flesh
wounds knit together
spitting metal into buildings

They yell at all this again, still they buy it
every time, yet to be a dancer
beginning forever backward
master of things unfolded

For Real This Time

Earth. We are no one.

Early life.
Visions of stale cola
in your narrow hand.
A somber room with curling
posters. That jacket makes
your legs look skinny.
Been running all night
can't stop puking.

Satan is just the possibility
of a baby inside me.
I remember the time
we spent sowing onions
under cemetery trees.
Buried a pocket knife
one for you, one for me.
Set fire to the dog.

Arching our backs in your closet
full ashtrays and bumblebees.
A crocheted shawl we found
hidden in the alley.
It belonged to a victim
we decided. A murder.
A Kidnapping, a beating.
It didn't matter. Now it's ours.
Smell here. Can you tell?

The last slide show

your uncle ever showed us
before he went to the hospital
and never came home
was about Israel.
Pictures of the desert. Dessert.
When could we get some of that
chocolate?
Is it real Israel? We would laugh.
Now they're all dead.

Not so funny
but the slide show was
painfully boring.
These kids who beg for death
jump on concrete.

Here or there
I wish you would
pack me up in your car and take me
like we did
the other day.
Only
for real this time.

To Be Truly Small

Get Small

I am the amoeba crawling backward
an empty telephone is my answer
to every tearful question hurled at the clouds
for every bullet caught or avoided

To be truly small is to ask for nothing
to accept the grab bag
someone else loaded
with no one in mind, only enemies

Sunset hill of banners that flip in the wind
ice angels prowl the span
woesome souls spread like fog
rows of caskets line the promontory

Cruelty field is rich with weeping flowers
drawn from crevices by the paling moon
mourning sun, cruelty canyon, cruelty meadow

Like wheat to the blacksmith
not food but a symbol of food, everyone laughing
this drink goes down like cherry wine
the more you get, the quicker you die.

Human Tiger Hero Born

Ice angels chase human design
sipping beer, chewing mint and coca
never leaving the bed.
Snow mounds outside the hotel.

But it's exactly the dark that snarls
and gapes with a windy tongue.
Unlit voices, true to nature
telling all, tapping at the window.

The legend of a circus creature
runs on all fours, walks on two.
Tearing into mischief from all sides
listens for objects that break into pieces.

Cures woes, cleans the wounded
saves carved paper pieces of our forebears
waiting for enemies, responsible to no one.
Please find me now. I am *down the hill.*

Newly Arrived, Dying

I awoke on the same island
I was born upon, Lesbos
we had been asleep, the both of us
for thousands of years
before the people came

Not destroyers, but builders
they came in droves
I told them that poetry
was born here

Sappho was our mother
they said, *bread shop here and housing here*
we will build it
you will see

Groping from an account of emptiness, they added
we drive tree river galaxies
only to die and to be born again
we must retake possession of the signs

Desert fathers of Nineveh
would never have predicted
the fate of this miraculous island city
on the brink of god, edge of death

They never got the chance
they were imprisoned, then swept
up to the mainland and scattered
so scattered

Religion wins with clouds of talons
riding the god train, flooded with men of understanding
yes they were we, I, you, it
dragging the sky down low

So let's say they take my lips away
they take my mouth away and what if
they take my brains away I will scream

With my skin and bathe
at the ancient cistern
of those who tried and died

My sister nation is every nation
the skies we share ring with such wild screams
not god now, but pain not love or understanding

A murdered "I" flits and crawls
the tip of a stem, receives the sun
dries her wings, leads her to daisies
where she injects her tongue

And nectar rushes
forth the flowers
drumbeats calling
bloom bloom bloom

ANACHRONIST

Love and Blood
Sonnet after Wyatt

And when one desires an introduction
of new blood to live yet without letting
such heated blood may deserve reduction
knowing pain is implicit and resist regretting.
The path to join blood could merit forgetting.
But life without blood is more difficult living
so drop the sanguine and begin forgiving.

To Such a Bird

Wyatt poem to the tune of "Ye Old Mule"

To such a bird, locked in your gilded cage
Hung high and displayed over newspaper page
It's sad your keeper views you only weekly
One hears your calls, but so obliquely.
Your forebears flew arcing trees of age.
Oh such a bird.

Your predicament would be hard to presage:
An imprisoned creature trapped on stage.
Memories of flight resurface sleekly
For such a bird.

The quiet times are a quiet rage
In front of audiences so disengaged.
The sun passes through your curtains meekly
Your colors faded; time passes bleakly.
Your feelings and feathers won't be assuaged
To such a bird.

Inviting a Friend to Supper
After Ben Jonson

This weekend eve, I implore your rev'rent
companionship to dine in decadence
within my candlelit rooms resplendent
where pleasant atmosphere does loom.
Long tables await, to carry our meal
and cushions beneath, to comfort your keel.
The lights will be perfect, the decor as well.
I will have my quartet play Pachelbel.
You needn't worry a stitch who'll be there
for I have only invited the fair,
the loyal, and most interesting folks
who have much to share and will laugh at your jokes.
Our guests are mostly of secretive sort
with spies and scoundrels, they'll never consort.
And more, they shan't mind if you lack habit
of dining on mutton or roast rabbit.
For there'll be loads of it, freshly prepared,
so bring with you the appetite of a bear.
To start, we'll have truffle slices on toast
and tapenade we had flown in from the coast.
Accompanied by vodka martinis
so dry, and rinsed in vermouth so cleanly
that nary the air of sweet will hover
above the glacial eau you'll discover
twirling amidst olives skew'rd on a point.
And if someone should offer you a joint,
you'll take or pass, according to your wish.
Beyond my walls, we are quiet as fish.
When our meal arrives you'll be astounded

at platters of game that ran unbounded
and veg'tables of varied color
to thrill the palate and hoist your humor.
Wild rice with plumes of steam will tantalize
and crusty breads will not just feast the eyes,
but comfort the soul. And when our meal ends,
we will have talked and enjoyed, made new friends;
delighted in each other and ourselves.
But before we grab our hats from the shelves
we'll relate stories of marvel and make
our way through scads of chocolaty cakes.
Fear not, my friend, for eats as these will not
give trouble of stomach nor waist one jot.
Now I'm certain you'll join our festival.
If you have any doubts, know you're special.
Given your nature, I'm sure you'll accept.
And given my own, know what to expect:
for knowing this is well-intentioned,
you'll forgive my fibbing the aforementioned.

Valediction Forbidding Mourning

After John Donne

Certain elder statesmen might pass
the last days of an elegant sojourn
with lov'd ones circling their stuffed sickbed
taking each hand in turn to say,

Tax not thy troubled front. Beg not
skyward for my protection. Now I
am off to better climes. Rest assured,
as will I, thy salty mist helps none.

So stay thy tears and know that I,
unlike some, shall return and must do.
Yes, as undoubtedly as two floating
magnets in a pool will run together,

so shall we. Wipe thine eyes and take
my hand, for I would have your company
as I board the train whereupon
I would kiss thee; enough to last

aeons. Being well beyond my absence
yet too meager for our union.
Feign not good cheer, but be it
and risk us minimal artifice.

Our verity will be the paste that sticks
us to the other no matter

how wide the map. For if we two
continents be, let it Asia and Africa,

Yin and Yang shaped, two parts of one,
where swarthy adept inhabitants
dwell within huts made of land. A land
as it is us, and binds us, despite oceans.

So stay thy tears, lest they loose
the train from its tracks. Saltwater
streams risk flooding the rails and could
rust the only tributary of my return.

Instead, visualize this: these tracks,
life and death, wrap the planet. Which
is best, 'cause once completed, they
form a loop! Be brave and look for me here.

The Dread That Would
Not Wait to Be Summoned

*Ronald McDonald is the Fifth Horseman
of the Apocalypse, in decasyllabic free verse.*

I saw it all with mine own inner eye;
it came 'pon me as the final horseman.
The horse it rode was taller than a house
whose each hoof splayed larger than an anvil.
The prints it made buried small children
helplessly drawn by its demonic wake.

Skies darkened and belched thunder and lightning.
The horseman's velocity slowed wind itself
and as he neared, I could make out his shape:
He was yellow armored, long and drawn out.
His helmet shone of vibrant red metal
despite the putrid air and sunless sky.

His face was pale and blanched like that of Death.
His nose was bulbous, crimson, and decayed.
His battle cry intoned pure insanity.
His arms, striped like those of a blood-letter,
waved flamboyantly; gesturing at nothing.
His mouth dripped blood red and his teeth were bared.

His steed leapt over streets, trees, and houses.
Children and simple-minded adults took pains
to gain proximity and to ingest
the following: from his person were flung
fried tubers, meat cakes dressed in wax paper,
and square tarts filled with sour fruit, drizzled in fat.

People fought and struggled with each other
over these products as they screamed wildly.
And I noticed this was what sustained them.
Their tongues lolled over it, suckling it,
as the horseman cackled relentlessly.
The people's bodies swelled and fell limp

as they died, soaking oils into the earth.
The final horseman's ammunition was
produced by machines that cook it all
in perfect symmetry; the goal of this
was not to promote longevity, but
specifically for culling their ducats.

And I saw the horseman rest by a tree.
And his followers drew close and frothing.
They tugged at the teats of his raging steed,
which indulged them all by showering forth
streams of frozen and darkly-colored milk.
They screamed and clamored; aching with delight.

The milk fell out and coagulated
in a heap faster than they could drink it;
from there emerged the first of his minions.
He rose from a cascade of slime, bearing
paper vessels for the crowd to carry
away their treasured personal servings.

The figure was tremendous of dimension;
where his master was gaunt and long of form
this one was of the opposite nature.
Immense yet squat, and colored like a bruise,

his body was covered in fur. His eyes
glared, staring into space, larger than plates.

This was not the last of the horseman's lackeys;
the unnamed dread borne of metal ovens.
He returned many times and does so still,
revealing at every turn new cohorts
and accomplices dealing curios
and deathblows to the unwitting people.

ZELIJ, A MAZE

Asassa Berberia
Woman Who Married the Mexican Carpenter

Take care, sweet woman
for the rings of riches
have a blood ruby punched into every one.

They fall continuously
tracing rivulets on the black mountain face
of human pain.

As with your hair.
Black at its heart
with red gold tints
highlighting a woven pattern

from years of work outdoors
with your hair plaited and uncovered.

But do take care
for you are a naked child in life.
One whose skin is pale
but blackened by the mountains above.

¡Asassa!
Your husband calls
from the next room and you arrive.
¡Can't you make me a spell
where the Patrón falls dead
and when his body stiffens
we get to bust it like a piñata
and all the jewels

fall out over the countryside
enough for us, enough for
everyone here!

Here
is not bad . . .
It is dark and dusty inside.
Your walls come straight out of the dirt.

Your forefathers built massive cities
from the mud of the Rif and Atlas ranges.
They crouch unchanged to this day.
Your ancestors also helped
the Arabs to navigate.

Today, Insh'allah,
you will help your husband
to be rid
of his boss.

Épaules de Brouillard

Épaules de brouillard marin sautent et marchent
en postures variées comme des immenses brigands
fantômes passants par le coin de moi
là où je suis écrasé par la mémoire de nous
tartiné au macadam des grosses avenues
de la ville que j'aurais quittée, rayons de l'aube
me rechauffent lentement en danger
touchant ma gueule à la rôtir
en symbole, en talisman, en torche debout
torche tombée, torche touché de torche
tronche de charbon
aux yeux de feux
étranger oublié

Sea Fog Shoulders
Tr. "Épaules de Brouillard"

Sea fog shoulders lumber in
various postures, oversized thieves
passing me as I lie here
crushed by the memory of us
spread across the asphalt
of the city I should have left long ago
dawn rays warming me slow, in danger
caressing my face, roasting it
I am the fallen torch, the torch touched
by a greater torch
charcoal head
eyes of fire
forgotten stranger

Qasida of Labid

Gone are these camps, smooth-floored
clear of tents and all that filled them.
Desolate the realm of the departed
brimming is the wind that rings of
war cataclysm and buoyant love months.

Beyond the mute or muting rock maze
clouds mumble and flash
percolating rain to feed our springs.
And so, this spread of verdant bushes
betrays the arid clay that clutches them.

How the gazelles dive across the planes
cataracting the air, cleaving the dusk
cutting the billowy horizon; honey-tinted
clouds blazing over a blue mirror
And how it all flows and pours amongst the rocks.

A few mules here show whipping scars.
They browse randomly over the herbage.
To give birth is to repurchase their past.
Their young yell and frolic in the wild
and reorient the elders to the land.

Stripped of humans, the deserted encampment
once again sings praises of itself in its own tongue.
But what of her, Nowara, who received your heart
and waited, but followed her people
so quietly we let the memory slip and so long ago?

Nowara the nimble youth whose feet
almond shape and color, coated with the fine dust
of the desert floor, carried her far beyond us
we racing the date arbors on festival day.
And she did grow to be a tender and noble woman

decorated in tresses, richness of eyes kohl-darkened
gold coins at her neck and breast.
It was to her we gave the soft red stone of our chest.
It was with her also that it finally fled
faded treasure, lapsed of time and patience.

Wine

Wine, you are fortunate
for the corks
ambling about your chest
were set high on the horizon

by water, sun, and fine parentage.
All bow to your dizzy highness.

When you are ready and sometimes
before you are ready
we flock to you
and your spicy overtones

to lie drunk, cradled in your recesses
succumbed to your dance
dreaming and forgetting
visions of conquest, defeat, and desire.

To cull you and crush you is all we ask!

Trampling your juices
sifting away your material skin
only amplifies your strength
and leaves us parched.

And at last when you air yourself
in the gloomy taverns
where you so commonly flow

your earthy pungency
the vines that built you
the wooden walls that held you

unleash a sensual monster
we can't escape
without being smitten into stupefaction.

Flies of Sidi-Harazem

Scat, you flies of Sidi-Harazem!
You brazen hags twirling idly in mid-air
lusting after rotted carrion fruits
finding only the flaky bones of my intentions
hurled over the rocky cliffs of your promises.

Scores of flies teem my windowsill horizon
clouding the walls and carrying away my memory
picking the teeth of my bedsprings
scouring the floors I stand on.

Lift me now, you trash eaters and thunder bugs!
Scoop me under a floating black puddle of your rickety bodies
all clinging and bumbling under the stress of your efforts.
Clean me if you must in your damnable fashion
lick me and dissolve me, but get me out of this prison.

The oil yards here billow death into the sky.
The railroads drill disease into our countryside.
The chemical plants crystallize the water they straddle
forcing it to crumble under its own weight
and the rivers are piling outside my window.

My stale sandwich gives you reason enough to breed.
My cell is a just carcass to house your young
writhing away in blind squirming piles, and like they are,
I am losing patience to be born into the rubble of the future

dying to live under the rotted umbrella of your city
killing away the mass of your progress

and within the currents of foul air that suspend us
obliterating your rosy measure of solution

overriding your tact and cunning
all dripping in finery and precision
abhorring any answers
rejecting solid builders.
We are the flies of Sidi-Harazem.

How the Sword Maiden
Loved a Young Man

Did you only see me as a body to satisfy your hunger
when you pulled me from the ocean, you knew I was far from home
swimming unprotected, in Morocco we never say
I have eaten enough today, please take my food
I have seen enough today, please take my freedom
I have lived enough today, please take my life

As I slid from the water to fill your cracked hands
I fought you like any maiden would, yes she would
tell you to go suck on a rotten rag, you maudlin child
you had no dexterity when you first held me, nor the last
little did we know we would spend the rest of our lives together

You brought your shiny treasure to the souk that morning
so proud to be seen with me, I was the beacon of your booth
they came and looked, you lost a button your chest was so big
no one minded my nose or how still I lay, dressing the ice
between lesser creatures, no one minded until the police noticed

They watched as we chatted and sold a few things
sitting around me and I saw, but said nothing
until they called the truck to drive through the stands
it followed them like a clanking impersonal storm cloud
I wondered what the driver had eaten that morning
certainly not me, certainly not you, ah but that truck

Would be eating more than its share soon
I called you in my language but you couldn't hear
as police asked you questions, people backed away

then earnest cries and tears began, I saw this too
before I was heaved into the truck with layers of garbage

I called and cried, you flew in head first
to help me, holding me in your arms, I stared into your neck
your pulse stopped as we hugged, the gears forced us closer
on the day we met we became one loving body, forever united
we had seen enough, eaten enough, lived enough together

Who could think we would ever say this, but we did
and the crowds could not believe it either
they too were crushed in the rubbish, rallied for days
forced together by the gears of governance, eyes full of pepper spray
everyone tearful, swimming the wishes of a fishmonger

May the skies one day ring with gold coins
forever turning, never falling, never dying

BRiAR & POND

Kohoutec

If the sky were a blown glass dome
tinted grey and glowing at the edge
broad and delicate
thin as a bubble and

If it would span the great thick
crust of the earth and
should the water of that earth
creep down a river, receding at one point
in the middle of it then

I would be a plump brown child
toasted by a series of days
near the equator
stretched out on said sandbar

Bloated on coconut milk
and drunk from the final sips
of everyone else's beer

After catapulting
down palm-arcaded highways
shifting gears from the passenger seat
of a yellow beetle.

From my sandbar I would see you
chalk mark in the brittle sky
silent and still
permanent and fleeting
flaring icy wanderer
unstoppable.

You and I Sipping Coffee

Only once I get there, the crows of culture
have eviscerated our Saturday afternoon
streets are slippery
with well-intentioned name calling

Nobel's nitro fortune benevolence
names the thrifty flavor of the month
branding intellectuals
feet cold on the drugstore floor, friends wait outside

Dead is clean in sun-soaked sheets
folded neatly, just for you to open
a package at the corner table
our neighborhood café

Dead is you and I sipping coffee
forever stepping through the cosmic door
in the wall behind those curtains
we ignored for years

This is the dead
right here among us waiting
faring well, traveling, observing
never commenting

Jaguar Mountain Trail

Young monks, burning stone
trample the blood path
up wet clay mountain

Whalen's verse, too eloquent
slid so easily from his wrists
his path will not be retraced

Here, the stone jaguar
jumps forest floors
branches lean aside
tears at the nimble doe

Fabled expression of fear
worn as a poet masque
canyon ribs daunting
soil as memory

Stomach of clay, weeping
bone pipe smoke the march
skeleton tune trail, poets born
mixing ink in a skull

What Makes a River Bleed

Can't help it if I think I'm falling.
This black tube will cancel regret
take it and heap it
over the bath walls.

Down through the drain tunnel
dark river spinning
wherever the tubes take me
once this tiny rock smashes me.

River take me to pieces
my invention is less than agile.
A monkey stays penniless
but richer than doves.

One's direction must be
different, so cared for by flowers.
Rocks forever collapse into new shapes
held fast against the river's draft.

Poem of the Tiny Power of Youth

*On the occasion of the birth of
my best friend's daughter*

oh, my
here and there was I looking
and never finding
until I discovered
that all there is to do is to look

and
by god's blood did I encounter
the girl of my dreams
flaming stone of my chest
guide to all things right

oh
your love could
hurt one so
I will call you Margaux
and nothing will prevent me
from protecting you ever

yes
forever

always

Poema del Pequenisimo Poder de la Juventud

*Con motivo del nacimiento de
la hija de mi mejor amigo*

¡ay!
busca aquí y allá
y no halla

entonces descubre que
no hay que a buscar

y
sangre de dios encuentra
la niña de mis sueños
piedra flamante de mi pecho
guía al derecho

¡ay!
tu amor puede doler tanto
te llamaré Margota
y nada me desbarata
de protegerte siempre

sí
siempre

eternamente

Idea for a Poem

Premise:
Water
swallows hard
and takes a look
deep within herself.

Conceit:
Water finds that her interior is the Sistine Chapel.

Aspects:

Water in the ocean—
Area of ceiling 1:
Heavenly skies (throughout)
Quality: Ether of Genesis
Color—Lapis Blue

Area of ceiling 2:
Descent into Hell
Qualities: Ocean depths, destroyer of things
Color—Black

Water in a river—
Area of ceiling:
The Flood
Qualities: Delivers nutrients to Earth, feeds Earth, washes
all away, the living and dead
Colors—Red, Gold, Brown

Water in a faucet—
Area of ceiling:

Congregation of waters/ Temptation and Expulsion
    from Eden
Qualities: Renewal, rebirth
Colors — Light Blue (of Zechariah's robe), Eggshell White
    (of architectural details)

Water in a vase —
    Area of the ceiling:
    Drunkenness of Noah
    Qualities: Misguided ego, trapped in excess
    Color — Yellow, burning Red of sun

Outcomes:
All earthly creatures invented themselves within Water and
    then left her.

Water eventually follows all earthly creatures and destroys
    them and what they have made.

I Paint Until The

figure I'm painting
comes fully to life
and demands
that I stop
touching it
with my
brush.

Clouds

Clouds are like friends.
Clouds are just like friends.
Clouds are just like friends. Exactly.
Clouds do what friends do. Every time.

Clouds either collect and block the sun or they pass by as they drop their shit on you, or maybe they hang around and drop their shit on you, or maybe the clouds don't show up at all. Ever.

Rarely will a cloud come to your rescue.

Clouds are also known to huddle and bounce colors of the setting sun.

An Earlier Time

I'm watching a program on a machine built at an earlier time.
The program is about an earlier time.

In that program, a woman is sitting
listening to a record that was made at an earlier time.

It can only be listened to on a facsimile
made at an earlier time
made to emulate another machine
built at an earlier time.

But the record, made at an earlier time
is older than the player
designed to play records from an earlier time.

On that record is classical music
recorded at an earlier time
written at an earlier time.

The classical music was based on a folk song
written at an earlier time.

That folk song recounted a story
or another song that
occurred at an earlier time.

SPILLING OVER

Sacred and Profane, Faceless Jacks

Haunting light under smoldering sun
faceless jacks a wet soupy melange
burnt out sky and constrained potential
canned by flat clouds and walled in
by the tarnished horizon
the human city is a multiplex concrete tomb

But desert valleys roll on forever
are motionless yet living
squirming yet frozen
time travelers yet solid
recording time
birthing humanity

Whereas our cities snuff it
without question, but the humans
rush to the city tomb and are blinded
by its artificial light, by everything it promises
everything hidden in its crevices
everything lit up in its store fronts
ducking between the thighs and the alleys

Of the city asphalt canals
this is where I find myself
when we are nothing but a buzz
a fragile tonal vibration
our false gods are lit up like tumbleweeds
starfish, frozen dinner dioramas
cardboard cutouts, eye shadow mascara
pink lip gloss, cotton candy flavored

Where humanity should have been
it was never seen
where love could have found its way
it was buried and these lights don't show me to you
they don't introduce you to me
instead, they erase me and they erase you
and these lights press us flat against the wall
of authoritarian control
in the light of the crooked window hills

But the arching sun drenched lands
of my mind give birth to life
let life free to spawn blinking
spider children riding the dust
civic petroglyphs of pain
these rocks tell no lies
this sand buries no truth

The dark only reveals the self to the self
it hides nothing
only in between spans of light
is reality allowed to freely express itself
to dance unhindered
in image, in dream, in truth, and symbol

To stay true, avoid the light
take the dark alley
take the graceful turn
take the steep curve off the Earth
and slide into the deepest river of sand
falling ever further
into the sun

Fripons Sans Visage

Tr. *Sacred and Profane, Faceless Jacks*

Lumière hantée d'un soleil ardent
fripons sans visage, jour bouée
ciel de charbon, potentiel limité
emboîté de sombres nuages, murés d'un horizon terni
la cité humaine est un tombeau multiplex rempli de bétons

Mais pourtant
les vallées du désert roulent éternellement
immobiles mais vivantes
tortillantes mais congelées
voyageuses cosmiques bien qu'ancrées
elles enregistrent l'histoire
elles font naître l'humanité

Alors que nos villes la détruisent
sans se poser de questions, les êtres humains
s'y précipitent à ce tombeau et s'y aveuglent
par sa lumière artificielle, par tout ce qu'elle promet
par tout caché dans ses crevasses
illuminé dans ces vitrines
planqué entre les cuisses et allées

Les canaux d'asphalte de centre ville
c'est là où je me retrouve, c'est là où je te vois
là où nous ne sommes plus rien qu'une murmure
nos faux dieux sont allumés comme des buissons brûlants, roulants
des étoiles de mers desséchées, diorama
de carton découpé, décoré en mascara, fard à paupières
lèvre rose, saveur brillante, barbe à papa

Là où l'humanité aurait du être
elle n'a jamais été vue
là, où l'amour aurait pu trouver son chemin
il a été enterré, et ces lumières ne me montrent pas à toi
elles ne te présentent pas à moi
au contraire elles nous effacent
et nous pressent à plat
contre le mur de contrôle autoritaire
au-dessus de cette lumière, s'imposent les monts carrés, fenêtrés

Mais ces terres trempées de soleil vivent
eternellement dans l'esprit, elles donnent naissance à la vie
elles la libèrent au vent pour se multiplier en clignotant
car nous ne sommes que des enfants d'araignées
montant des plumes de poussière
en passant des pétrographes civiques de douleur
ces rochers qui ne racontent jamais des mensonges
et cette sable qui n'enterrera jamais la vérité

Car l'abîme ne fait que révéler le soi à soi
elle ne cache rien
seulement entre les deux travées de jour
somme nous enfin permis de nous exprimer
à danser sans inquiétude
en rêve, en vérité, en symbole

D'être un vrai être, on doit éviter la lumière
prendre la ruelle plus sombre
le virage elegant
la courbe abrupte de la Terre
et suivre la plus profonde
des rivières de sable, en tombant
toujours plus proche
au soleil

Coney Island Siren

Gentle are the twisting tides
boiling and heaving, folding in pressure.
Awesome tanks of deep gather overhead
to foster meager thoughts.

Here, among the sea crags
struggling past scattered ideas
dull glitter in the quivering light
have I made my home.

A summons, a broken cry
from the sheltering density
a meek yet penetrating voice
has brought me here to drift.

I cannot hear it nor can I stop listening
yet the message is not lost
I tumble unguided, swept over mute valleys
obscure mountains and maligned seabeds.

The sliver of me recalls
the sound of you
summoning me again
from this ocean.

There's something about
memory...
What is a memory anyway?

The ship in my chest
has sunk once more
and I walk to shore
to find you.

And your earth is so native
of flesh, so foreign of region
so ruptured of borders
so elusive
of arms

that I am dissolved into mist
and born again
forgetting what it was
forgetting why again I was summoned
erasing
my spirit.

I am again
and I am man again
and we are together
and I am your father
and I am my father
and I can't hold you close enough
and I must do this thing right.

Sweet dreams of
deep remorse
haunt my sleep
are the plague of my steps.

Past the noise of stamping feet
and the creaking wooden pit that surrounds me

are the gasps and groans
of chanting demons, wheezing dour airs
intoning madness, agony, and deceit.

They rob the final bits of my memory.
My trust in a liar has buried me here
and the crowds laugh at my predicament.

Memory.
What was memory anyway.
I forget…
I forget me and I forget about you
and I forget what brought me here.
I forget how to escape.
Was I your memory of me
were you my memory of you
or was I dreaming my remembering?

So much drowning
so much sorrow
so much escaping
and so much running.

And so little dreaming.
I forget that I am dreaming and running
I forget where to go
I forget what I am dreaming about
and what I am running for
where I am running to.

I have to get you back
to do right by you
this must be why you have summoned me

but I lose track in these sheltered alleys
I can't see straight because my eyes
are dry and crusting…
Who were you to me again
and where were we going anyway?

I should have known it wasn't you.
This is only my vision, my delusion.
You were never meant to stay by my side
you were made by me but also made to leave me.
Knowing this breaks my heart
I see you walking alone
but your path is not a lonely one
your path is your own, and you shall carve it
my mistakes and my visions were mine all along.

Is it you I see ahead or the memory
of what I could have meant to you?
I will do it all again
Your name
you are of the earth
and I the craggy twig
that dropped you…
The air of the surface forest
is so hot I am gasping.

I am looking for you again.
I think I remembered you once
a daughter.
My sweet, lost, my only daughter.
The ocean of trees is so dry
I am not certain of anything
this light shows me.

But, I can see it
it is you
this, here, this was you
and we loved each other
and I made sure you were safe
I made sure you were so...safe.

Steep ribbons of clay beneath me
turn into warm sand
and I am home again
the only home I can remember.
The day's events softly turning
muffled by the shuddering sea.

With a sigh, the sea wonders
when I'll throw myself into it.
Scaly back of ocean rolling.

Lips and teeth continually gnashing
I consider my last sentence spoken
strong medicines slide through my blood
they pulse in my head, exposing my circuitry
full bore to the end.

In the end
it is always ever blinded
we pulling on oars or swimming
barrel-chested and shivering
reaching, yet hurled ever further.

In the end
is this how it ends?
Once hidden within the foaming drapery

a derelict memory arises
and at last I know
what I was supposed to do.

If you should summon me again
I promise to do right by you
my lost little siren
and I will not be tempted
by that terrible thirst
brought on by the sea.

I hush, slumped and drawn
into a pit of flotsam.
A sailor's life is a jail forever
if between his ears.

I call the wrath of slimy gods of the deep
to drown me in their hidden water.

ABOUT THE POET

PHOTO: Sofia Leisou, Heartmade Arts, Corfu, Greece

YOUSSEF ALAOUI is a Moroccan Latino American poet, author, editor and artist. Alaoui studied classical Arabic and Spanish baroque poetry, and Moroccan contemporary poetry at New College of California, San Francisco. He has spent most of his professional life in library stacks and at the computer referencing facts and citations, and for a few years, served as a contracted international investigator. Alaoui's work has appeared in *Exquisite Corpse, Big Bridge, Cherry Bleeds, 580 Split, Full of Crow, Virgogray Poetry, Dusie Press, Tsunami Books, Red Fez,* and *Rivet Journal.* He is also the editor and designer for the books *Murder* (2013), *Cineplex* (2014), *Notes From An Orgy* (2014), *poems about something & nothing* (2015), served as editor of the anthology, *Lost Frames Compendium of Poetry and Art (2015),* and did layout and design for *Invisible Idylls: A Romantic Extravagance, for John Seaver* (2013). He is the author of the novella, *The Blue Demon* (2012), *Death at Sea — Poems* (2013), and the short story collection, *Fiercer Monsters (2017)*. Alaoui, a Pushcart Prize nominee, is the founder of Paper Press Books & Assoc. Publishing Company and the Beast Crawl Poetry Festival. His home cities are Morro Bay, Tempe, Paris, Lille, Seattle, and Oakland. youssefalaoui.tumblr.com. ✸

OTHER BOOKS BY
2LEAF PRESS

2LEAF PRESS challenges the status quo by publishing alternative fiction, non-fiction, poetry and bilingual works by activists, academics, poets and authors dedicated to diversity and social justice with scholarship that is accessible to the general public. 2LEAF PRESS produces high quality and beautifully produced hardcover, paperback and ebook formats through our series: *2LP Explorations in Diversity, 2LP University Books, 2LP Classics, 2LP Translations, Nuyorican World Series,* and *2LP Current Affairs, Culture & Politics.* Below is a selection of 2LEAF PRESS' published titles.

2LP EXPLORATIONS IN DIVERSITY
Substance of Fire: Gender and Race in the College Classroom
by Claire Millikin
Foreword by R. Joseph Rodríguez, Afterword by Richard Delgado
Contributed material by Riley Blanks, Blake Calhoun and Rox Trujillo

Black Lives Have Always Mattered
A Collection of Essays, Poems, and Personal Narratives
Edited by Abiodun Oyewole

The Beiging of America:
Personal Narratives about Being Mixed Race in the 21st Century
Edited by Cathy J. Schlund-Vials, Sean Frederick Forbes and Tara Betts
with an Afterword by Heidi Durrow

What Does it Mean to be White in America?
Breaking the White Code of Silence, A Collection of Personal Narratives
Edited by Gabrielle David and Sean Frederick Forbes
Introduction by Debby Irving and Afterword by Tara Betts

2LP UNIVERSITY BOOKS
Designs of Blackness, Mappings in the Literature and Culture of African Americans
A. Robert Lee
20TH ANNIVERSARY EXPANDED EDITION

2LP CLASSICS
Adventures in Black and White
Edited and with a critical introduction by Tara Betts
by Philippa Schuyler
Monsters: Mary Shelley's Frankenstein and Mathilda
by Mary Shelley, edited by Claire Millikin Raymond

2LP TRANSLATIONS
Birds on the Kiswar Tree
by Odi Gonzales, Translated by Lynn Levin
Bilingual: English/Spanish

Incessant Beauty, A Bilingual Anthology
by Ana Rossetti, Edited and Translated by Carmela Ferradáns
Bilingual: English/Spanish

NUYORICAN WORLD SERIES
Our Nuyorican Thing, The Birth of a Self-Made Identity
by Samuel Carrion Diaz, with an Introduction by Urayoán Noel
Bilingual: English/Spanish

Hey Yo! Yo Soy!, 40 Years of Nuyorican Street Poetry,
The Collected Works of Jesús Papoleto Meléndez
Bilingual: English/Spanish

LITERARY NONFICTION
No Vacancy; Homeless Women in Paradise
by Michael Reid

The Beauty of Being, A Collection of Fables, Short Stories & Essays
by Abiodun Oyewole

WHEREABOUTS: Stepping Out of Place,
An Outside in Literary & Travel Magazine Anthology
Edited by Brandi Dawn Henderson

PLAYS
Rivers of Women, The Play
by Shirley Bradley LeFlore, with photographs by Michael J. Bracey

AUTOBIOGRAPHIES/MEMOIRS/BIOGRAPHIES
Trailblazers, Black Women Who Helped Make America Great
American Firsts/American Icons
by Gabrielle David

Mother of Orphans
The True and Curious Story of Irish Alice, A Colored Man's Widow
by Dedria Humphries Barker

Strength of Soul
by Naomi Raquel Enright

Dream of the Water Children:
Memory and Mourning in the Black Pacific
by Fredrick D. Kakinami Cloyd
Foreword by Velina Hasu Houston, Introduction by Gerald Horne
Edited by Karen Chau

The Fourth Moment: Journeys from the Known to the Unknown, A Memoir
by Carole J. Garrison, Introduction by Sarah Willis

POETRY
PAPOLÍTICO, Poems of a Political Persuasion
by Jesús Papoleto Meléndez
with an Introduction by Joel Kovel and DeeDee Halleck

Critics of Mystery Marvel, Collected Poems
by Youssef Alaoui, with an Introduction by Laila Halaby

shrimp
by jason vasser-elong, with an Introduction by Michael Castro
The Revlon Slough, New and Selected Poems

by Ray DiZazzo, with an Introduction by Claire Millikin
Written Eye: Visuals/Verse
by A. Robert Lee

A Country Without Borders: Poems and Stories of Kashmir
by Lalita Pandit Hogan, with an Introduction by Frederick Luis Aldama

Branches of the Tree of Life
The Collected Poems of Abiodun Oyewole 1969-2013
by Abiodun Oyewole, edited by Gabrielle David
with an Introduction by Betty J. Dopson

2Leaf Press is an imprint owned and operated by the Intercultural Alliance
of Artists & Scholars, Inc. (IAAS), a NY-based nonprofit organization that
publishes and promotes multicultural literature.

NEW YORK
www.2leafpress.org